My Bar/Bat Mitzvah

A Memory and Keepsake Journal

By Edward Hoffman, Ph.D.

CHRONICLE BOOKS

San Francisco

My Bar/Bat Mitzvah

A Memory and Keepsake Journal

ISBN 0-8118-4594-X

Design by Efrat Rafaeli
Illustrations by Leigh Wells
Manufactured in China

Distributed in Canada by
Raincoast Books
9050 Shaughnessy Street
Vancouver, B.C. V6P 6E5

10 9 8 7 6 5 4 3 2 1

Chronicle Books LLC
85 Second Street
San Francisco, CA 94105
www.chroniclebooks.com

To Neal, friend and colleague

contents

Mazel Tov

מזל טוב

Mazel tov! You have reached one of your life's most important Jewish steps—becoming a *bar* or *bat mitzvah* (literally, "son or daughter of the commandment"). Though your birth certainly gave joy to your parents, grandparents, and others connected to them, all you really had to do back then was appear. This time it's very different. You're the star of attention once again, but you're now mastering words and ideas that come from Judaism's 4,000-year-old history. And certainly, while you may have enjoyed past birthdays and synagogue activities, this event is like no other.

You are now vitally linked to an ancient tradition—Jewish sages have long viewed the age of 13 for boys and 12 for girls as having important religious status. In the second century CE, Rabbi Eleazar ben Simeon wrote that a father is responsible for his son's deeds until the age of 13. The *Pirkei Avot* (Ethics of our Fathers), a book of Jewish wisdom, taught that "at five a boy is ready to study Torah, at ten . . . to study Mishnah, and at 13 . . . to be responsible for the mitzvot." As far back as 2,000 years ago, Jewish males at age 13 were authorized to participate as adults in all synagogue ceremonies and even legal matters.

Where did this viewpoint originate? Probably from the Bible, which reports that Abraham was 13 years old when he rejected his father's idols and that twins Jacob and Esau at this same age went their separate ways. In Jerusalem during the time of the Second Temple, the rabbis would customarily bless a boy who successfully completed his first day of fasting for Yom Kippur at age 12 or 13.

What about Jewish girls? Throughout most of Jewish history, women's roles were valued more in the home than in the synagogue, and women did not commonly attend synagogue alongside men until the last century. So the bat mitzvah celebration for girls is a more recent tradition, officially introduced in France and Italy sometime in the last 200 years and later adopted in other countries. In the past 30 or 40 years, bat and bar mitzvahs have become equal in most branches of Judaism. Today, both boys and girls receive synagogue *aliyot*, chant the *haftarah*, give a *derashah* (Torah talk), and enjoy festive family meals or parties.

Of course, being a bar or bat mitzvah does not mean you're now an adult in *all* aspects of your life. Though you may have your own cell phone and computer, your development is still unfinished emotionally, spiritually, and even physically—you'll be steadily growing up for a while. And even when physical changes stop, your inner growth will certainly continue. Millennia ago, our sages spoke to this. As Rabbi Judah ben Temah said: "At 30, one reaches full strength, and at 40, one reaches understanding; at 50, one is able to give counsel, and at 60, one reaches maturity."

So what's *really* different? Something truly exciting and momentous: You've gained your Jewish responsibility as an adult. In learning right from wrong, studying Judaism, and performing rituals and good deeds, you now carry just as much importance as those of older generations did. In this respect, you have truly reached a key spiritual place in your Jewish life.

Life is meant to be celebrated, and your bar or bat mitzvah is an especially wonderful celebration. Though you may not know it now, it will evoke beautiful memories for many years to come—even as you get older and are one day blessed to experience this vital Jewish event as a parent, aunt, uncle, or grandparent yourself.

This book is designed for precisely this purpose—to provide a snapshot of you, your life, and your feelings about your Jewish adulthood at this special time. Memory is a valuable thing in the Jewish tradition; it connects us to sacred moments of the past and simultaneously serves as a map and compass for the future. In the pages that follow, you'll find space to write about, reflect on, and gather memories of the best things in your life, as well as your hopes, dreams, and plans for years ahead. The contents of this journal will become an essential part of what your bar or bat mitzvah is all about and will strengthen and honor diverse memories around it.

Albert Einstein once said, "There are only two ways to live your life. One is as though nothing is a miracle. The other is that everything is." Your bar or bat mitzvah is more than a blessing—it's a bit miraculous. So celebrate it as fully as you can, using this journal to Jewishly preserve that joyful spirit.

Translation note:
When translating traditional Hebrew sources, the aim has been to use gender-neutral language yet also honor the original meaning of the text.

your family tree

"Honor your father and your mother." —Exodus 20:12

Your family is the foundation of your Jewish life. For more than 4,000 years, respecting and caring for family members has been among Judaism's highest values, and our spiritual leaders have always insisted that we treat everyone in our families with compassion and dignity. "When a person honors one's mother and father," the Babylonian Talmud observes, "God says, 'It is as though I had dwelled among them and they had honored me.'" Some sacred books are even filled with specific instructions for fulfilling our family obligations, depending on the age and health of our relatives.

"Judaism is a family religion," comments Paul Palnik, a leader in Jewish art education. "It's all about the marvelous adventures of Abraham and Sarah, and their descendants through the ages. Our sages have always viewed the Jewish people as one big family and embraced converts as newcomers to it."

The Bible's first book, Genesis, focuses vividly on family life—including both the joys and challenges of relating to parents, children, brothers, and sisters. "Be fruitful and multiply" is likewise God's prime commandment to Adam and Eve—a commandment that highlights the importance of child-raising as a vital spiritual activity.

And though we're encouraged to aim for holiness, we are also not expected to attain perfection in others or ourselves. Familiar Biblical family struggles of our patriarchs and matriarchs—Jacob with his twin Esau, Joseph with his eleven brothers, Leah with her sister Rachel, and even Moses with his older siblings Aaron and Miriam—make this point clear. Palnik adds, "The Hebrew Bible's emphasis on the family teaches children that there are no perfect people. Rather, we have to learn to love the people in our family—and later others too—despite their imperfections. This is the key to living Jewishly in the real, not fantasy, world."

Your family will no doubt play a crucial role as you become a bar or bat mitzvah, whether by helping you rehearse and learn your Torah portion, making plans for celebrating the occasion, or just being there to talk to if things seem overwhelming and like you'll never get through it all. Here's some space to remember your family at this moment in your life.

live and learn

Use the family tree to fill in the names of family members and where they were born. Your parents and grandparents are great resources if you're unsure of all the names from the past.

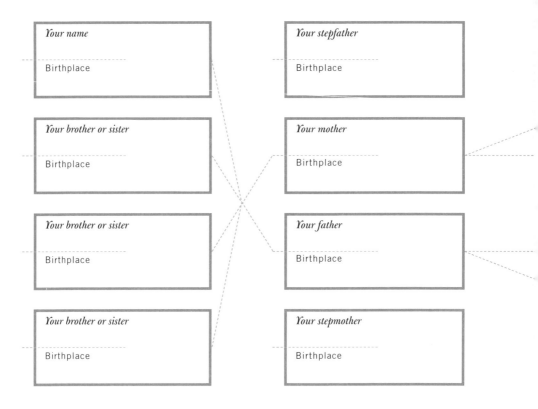

Your name

Birthplace

Your brother or sister

Birthplace

Your brother or sister

Birthplace

Your brother or sister

Birthplace

Your stepfather

Birthplace

Your mother

Birthplace

Your father

Birthplace

Your stepmother

Birthplace

Your maternal great grandmother

Birthplace

Your maternal great grandfather

Birthplace

Your maternal grandmother

Birthplace

Your maternal great grandmother

Birthplace

Your maternal grandfather

Birthplace

Your maternal great grandfather

Birthplace

Your paternal grandmother

Birthplace

Your paternal great grandmother

Birthplace

Your paternal grandfather

Birthplace

Your paternal great grandfather

Birthplace

Your paternal great grandmother

Birthplace

Your paternal great grandfather

Birthplace

Your cousin

Your maternal aunt

Your cousin

Your maternal uncle

Your cousin

Your cousin

Your maternal aunt

Your cousin

Your maternal uncle

Your cousin

Your cousin

Your maternal aunt

Your cousin

Your maternal uncle

Your cousin

Your paternal aunt

Your paternal uncle

Your cousin

Your cousin

Your cousin

Your paternal aunt

Your paternal uncle

Your cousin

Your cousin

Your cousin

Your paternal aunt

Your paternal uncle

Your cousin

Your cousin

Your cousin

more about your family

My sister

What I like most about her

My sister

What I like most about her

My sister

What I like most about her

My brother

....

What I like most about him

....

....

....

....

My brother

....

What I like most about him

....

....

....

....

My brother

....

What I like most about him

....

....

....

My mom

....

What I admire most about my mom

....

....

....

....

....

....

....

My dad

....

What I admire most about my dad

....

....

....

....

....

....

....

....

If you are blessed to have living grandparents, what do you admire most about each of them? Write something specific about their personalities.

My grandmother

What I like about my grandmother

What I call her (Bubbie, Nana, Grandma, for example)

My grandfather

What I like about my grandfather

What I call him (Zaida, Papa, Grampy, for example)

My grandmother

....

What I like about my grandmother

....

....

....

....

....

What I call her

....

My grandfather

....

What I like about my grandfather

....

....

....

....

....

What I call him

....

If you have any grandparents who are no longer living, but whom you remember, write something about them, too:

In your opinion, which family member's personality is most like your own?

Who do you think you look the most like?

What's different about you from the rest of your family?

If you become a parent one day, what would you wish most for your own child?

Paste or draw a picture of family members here.

your Jewish birthday

"Teach us to number our days." —Psalms 90:12

יום הולדת

Did you know that you have a special Jewish birthday, totally separate from your secular one? It's likely one of the reasons why your official bar or bat mitzvah date is probably different from your "regular" birthday. For instance, if you were born on June 1, your bar or bat mitzvah officially almost certainly falls either earlier or later in our secular calendar.

Why? The Hebrew calendar—which dates back more than two millennia—is based on the moon's rotation around the earth. One rotation takes 29.5 days. Each Hebrew month is counted as either 29 or 30 days, and 12 of them make a year. As the ancient rabbis saw, the big problem is that these lunar months add up to only about 354 days: eleven days short of our solar year of 365 days.

Therefore, if we hadn't adjusted the Hebrew calendar to match the solar calendar, Rosh Hashanah and all the other Jewish holidays would wander around the solar year. In one year they might all be in winter, and a few years later, in summer. Since several holidays celebrate harvests and are tied to the Holy Land's seasons, not adjusting the calendar would cause an awkward situation—it would seem silly to celebrate the fall harvest (*Sukkot*) in early spring.

To solve this problem, the rabbis cleverly created a Jewish leap year containing an additional month—known as *Adar 2*—placed sometime after the regular late-winter month of *Adar*. The Hebrew leap year occurs roughly every two or three years. So in any particular Hebrew year, each holiday—as well as your own birthday—will fall "early" or "late" in relation to the matching solar year. Jewish mystics teach that each Hebrew month has a special spiritual theme that guides us during the year and that our birth month shows our personal strengths and challenges in life.

the Hebrew months

Month	Tribe of Israel	Symbol	Words to Live By
Tishrei	Ephraim	Bull	Welcome new things into your life
Cheshvan	Menasheh	Eagle or unicorn	Create a good habit
Kislev	Benjamin	Wolf	Know your dreams
Tevet	Dan	Serpent	Overcome your anger
Shevat	Asher	Olive tree	Appreciate your food
Adar	Naftali	Deer	Laugh and be joyful
Nissan	Judah	Lion	Speak clearly
Iyar	Issachar	Donkey	Think deeply
Sivan	Zevulun	Fish	Listen to others
Tammuz	Reuven	Water	Be realistic
Av	Shimon	A building	Be more generous
Elul	Gad	Goat	Learn to be still

live and learn

Your Hebrew birthday, month, and year — your parents or your rabbi can help you figure out the date if you are unsure:

Your secular birthday, month, and year:

What is the Hebrew date of your bar or bat mitzvah?

What is the secular date of your bar or bat mitzvah?

How do you relate the "words to live by" and the Israeli tribe associated with your birth month to your everyday life?

You now

Paste a picture of yourself here—just a regular one, for a record of your everyday life at 12 or 13.

You during one of your previous birthdays

Paste a picture from a past birthday celebration here—it can be one from any birthday you like.

your Hebrew name

"These are the names of the children of Israel." —Exodus 1:1

Have you ever wondered about your Hebrew name and where it came from? Jewish boys are given their Hebrew names as part of the *bris* ceremony when they are eight days old, and most Jewish girls receive theirs at a baby-naming ceremony. The name given may be Hebrew, Yiddish, or a combination of both. The Kabbalah—Judaism's mystical tradition—teaches that one's Hebrew name is linked to one's soul, so there's more to a name than just being what someone calls when dinner is ready.

All Hebrew names have a meaning, such as Ruth ("companion") or Samuel ("God has dedicated"), and their spellings and even numerical values are important. By adding up the numbers represented by each of the letters of your Hebrew name, you get a total number—which then relates to various Hebrew words in different arrangements. Practitioners of Kabbalah believe that finding all the possibilities in your Hebrew name can provide an alternate, secret pathway to God.

For Jews today, Biblical names—like David and Ruth—remain popular and meaningful, providing a connection to illustrious figures of our ancient past, as well as the more recent generations, that bore those names—such as the Israeli leader David Ben Gurion and the U.S. Supreme Court justice Ruth Bader Ginsburg.

Often Jewish children are named after an honored family member who has passed away, such as a grandparent or other close relative. Sometimes the Jewish name doesn't exactly match the English name (the initial letter usually being consistent), but parents often prefer to use the same or a similar name—such as the English *Jeremy* and the Hebrew *Yirmeyahu*, which are versions of the Biblical name *Jeremiah*. Orthodox Jews and Israelis today often give their children Hebrew names that are used for both everyday and religious purposes.

the Hebrew alphabet

א	Aleph	1
ב	Beit	2
ג	Gimel	3
ד	Daled	4
ה	Hei	5
ו	Vov	6
ז	Zaiyin	7
ח	Chet	8
ט	Tet	9
י	Yud	10
כ	Kaf	20
ל	Lamed	30
מ	Mem	40
נ	Nun	50
ס	Samech	60
ע	Ayin	70
פ	Pei	80
צ	Tzadi	90
ק	Kuf	100
ר	Reish	200
ש	Shin	300
ת	Tav	400

live and learn

What is your Hebrew name?

What does your Hebrew name mean?

After whom were you named?

Where was this person born and where did he or she grow up?

What's an interesting fact about his or her life?

How are you similar to the person you were named for?

Does your Hebrew name originally come from a person in the Bible or somebody else in Jewish history? If so, which one and why was he or she famous?

honoring your teachers and mentors

"Who is wise? One who learns from everyone." —*Pirkei Avot*

מורים

Everyone growing up is guided by teachers, to whom the Jewish tradition gives great respect. Whether they help us to learn about the world or about our Jewish heritage, they can have big effects on our early lives. Long after notebooks and class schedules have faded, there's no doubt you'll always remember a favorite teacher who sparked a youthful interest into a career or lifelong hobby, or one who just inspired or motivated you in a particular way.

Judaism teaches that learning is a continual, lifelong process, no matter our age or background. It's said that Rabbi Akiva—among the greatest of all sages—as a poor shepherd began to study only at the age of 40. Jews have long been known as the "People of the Book"; desire for learning is a basic and integral part of our religion. It's not surprising that Rabbi Joshua ben Parachia long ago advised, "Get yourself a teacher and acquire unto yourself an associate, and judge *all* in the scale of merit." Rabbi Joseph ben Joezer likewise suggested, "Let your house be a meeting place for the wise . . . and drink in their words with thirst."

Our sages emphasized that we can also learn important things from people who are not necessarily our classroom teachers. In the past, they were often older relatives such as uncles, aunts, grandparents, family friends, and neighbors who imparted wisdom—and sometimes livelihood and domestic skills—to Jewish boys and girls. Often the entire extended family lived in the same city and could offer frequent guidance.

Though today relatives and friends often live far away from one another, it's easier than ever before—thanks to e-mail and other modern forms of communication—to remain close. Because we can get knowledge and advice from almost anyone, anywhere, nowadays, our learning can truly be global. What an amazing opportunity.

live and learn

Who have been your three favorite teachers so far in your school career? What subjects do they teach?

1
Subject:

2
Subject:

3
Subject:

What was special about each of them?

1

2

3

Name another older person, such as a camp counselor, family friend, or neighbor, who taught you something helpful.

What did this person show or teach you that has been valuable to you?

Have you been a "teacher," tutor, or mentor to a younger person, imparting a new skill to a sibling, relative, or friend? If so, who was it, and what did you teach?

----

knowing your friends

"Even in Heaven, it's good to have a friend." —*Yiddish proverb*

חברים

Judaism regards friends as among life's greatest treasures. They make us laugh when we're sad, give us advice when we're confused, and make good times even better. Such things are truly terrific. But our tradition also teaches—perhaps even more importantly—that friendship helps us to become kinder, more caring people.

How? By learning to appreciate other people's feelings and to prize them as our own. Our hearts open and compassion flowers with friends. When good friends enrich our lives, we don't worry so much about ourselves all the time. We become less self-centered, less concerned about our own desires, wants, and disappointments. Without friends we can certainly survive physically, but our days become colder and more selfish without their presence. "Friends in this life," reveals a proverb from the Kabbalah, "were souls who once sat together in Paradise."

Jewish sages also saw laughter as a wonderful—even spiritual—quality we can bring to others. In their longstanding view, helping someone to laugh was no trivial matter; it could even be a blessing. Certainly this tradition has borne its legacy on the many famous comedians that have come from Jewish backgrounds.

In a beautiful Talmudic tale, Rabbi Beroka one day found himself in the marketplace in the Persian city of Be Lefet. We're not told so, but maybe he was feeling lonely or sad. Suddenly, the prophet Elijah appeared to him. The rabbi asked him: "Is there anyone in this marketplace who deserves a place in the World-to-Come?" Elijah answered, "No."

A short time later, two seemingly ordinary men walked by. Elijah told the rabbi, "These men deserve a place in the World-to-Come." When Rabbi Beroka eagerly asked their occupation, they replied: "We are comedians, and we cheer up those who are depressed. And whenever we see two people quarreling, we work hard to make peace between them."

Sharing fun and laughter with friends isn't the only thing important in life, but as this ancient story suggests, it's certainly among them. And, who knows, if you're fortunate like Rabbi Beroka was, some day the prophet Elijah may show you this personally.

live and learn

Who were your friends that came to your bar or bat mitzvah?

1
2
3
4
5
6
7
8
9
10
11
12
13
14
15
16
17
18
19
20

Name things you like about some of your friends.

1   Who

     What I like

2   Who

     What I like

3   Who

     What I like

4   Who

     What I like

5   Who

     What I like

6   Who

     What I like

Which friends came from far away? Who came the farthest and from where?

1 ....
2 ....
3 ....
4 ....
5 ....
6 ....

Different people become good friends for different reasons—one may excel at your favorite sport; one might make hilarious jokes; one may share a special interest you have. Name three things that are important to you in the friendships you have.

1 ....
....
....

2 ....
....
....

3 ....
....
....

"To have a friend, be a friend" is an old saying. Do you think it's true? Why do your friends like you? What makes you a unique friend?

knowing your heroes

"Who is honored? One who honors other people." —Pirkei Avot

גבורים

Making the world a better place is one of Judaism's top values. Every one of us is encouraged—even expected—when we reach religious adulthood to contribute to humanity's big mission. But for people at any age, it's not always an easy thing. Sometimes we're not exactly sure how to help, or even how to decide what really needs our action. Our sages have always emphasized the importance of having personal heroes who guide and inspire us. In countless Jewish writings, *tzaddikim* (righteous persons) are praised as beacons who light up our paths.

Some figures can come from the Bible—such as Abraham and Sarah; Moses and his siblings; King David and his son Solomon; Esther and Mordechai; Ruth; and many others. But far more ordinary folks—including those we know in our everyday lives—can also be our heroes. They can be teachers, rabbis and cantors, neighbors, and merchants—from almost every walk of life.

So what makes people heroes? In the Jewish tradition, what makes a hero involves some specific things, but with one great commonality: A hero must be someone who helps other people. In doing so, the hero helps humanity approach a more divine state. As Rabbi Nachman of Bratslav said two centuries ago, "The world says that you should not seek greatness. But I say that you should seek *only* greatness—the greatest possible *tzaddik*."

In contemporary life, the Jewish educator Danny Siegel has written many books for teens that discuss heroes in action today. In virtually every community, large and small, these heroes quietly perform good deeds that truly make a difference.

live and learn

Who are two famous people today whom you admire?

1

2

What do you most admire about each one?

1

2

In Jewish history, who are two people whom you admire?

1

2

What do you most admire about each one?

1

2

Now, name someone living today not famous at all whom you admire.

What do you most admire about this person?

What can you do to be more like this person?

protecting nature and animals

"A righteous person knows the needs of animals." —Proverbs 12:10

Almost everyone today is interested in protecting the environment. Did you know that it's been a Jewish value for thousands of years? Long before dwindling natural resources caused people to support nature, Judaism emphasized this view. It's even found in the Ten Commandments, in number four: "The seventh day is a Sabbath onto the Lord your God; you shall not do any work, you, your son or daughter, your male or female servant, *or your cattle*." Everyone, even animals, deserves a day off his or her feet. Many employers even as recently as the early 1900s expected *workers* to toil every day of the week, so the ancient concern for animals is even more remarkable.

The Torah offers plenty of guidelines for treating animals kindly. One of the original 613 *mitzvot* says, "You shall not plow with an ox and a mule together," since both animals—being of unequal size and strength—would suffer from the imbalance. The Talmud forbids us to eat a meal before feeding our animals and from acquiring a domestic animal or bird unless we can feed it properly. Later, in the Middle Ages, the Book of the Righteous advised that "a good person does not sell his beast to one who is cruel."

Kindness to animals is no small thing. In the Bible, God selected Moses to lead our people out of Egyptian slavery not because he was strong or smart, but because he was such a caring shepherd. When God saw Moses carrying on his shoulders a tired young sheep back to its flock, God said, "Because you tend the sheep belonging to humans with such mercy, by your life I swear you shall be the shepherd of My sheep, Israel."

Though Jews have been forced to wander through many lands, honoring the environment has been vital to our tradition. Several holidays, like Tu B'Shevat and Sukkot, celebrate trees and flowering plants. Others relate to the ripening of fruit and the harvesting of grain. Though most Jewish people no longer live in the Holy Land, these observances make us truly respect nature as God's creation. Today, in a world with more than six billion people, it's more important than ever to have this awareness.

live and learn

Has anything that you have learned in your bar or bat mitzvah studies heightened your awareness of the world around you?

What are some things you can do to contribute to the protection and stewardship of both the earth and animals after your bar or bar mitzvah?

Do you now have a pet? If not, have you ever had one?
If so, what kind(s) and what are their names?

What do you like most about having a pet?

How has having a pet made you a more caring person?

Do you know how animals are killed in a kosher way to avoid needless pain? What does this mean to you?

Paste or draw a picture of your pet(s) here.

tzedakah: giving to charity

"Tzedakah is equal to all the other commandments combined."
—*The Talmud*

To be a charitable person is one of Judaism's highest values. We are told that Abraham and Sarah—who God chose to begin the Jewish people—always kept their tent open to strangers weary for food, drink, and companionship. Such hospitality was basic to a righteous life. Ever since, for more than 4,000 years, our tradition has been filled with concern for helping those less fortunate than ourselves. The Bible, Talmud, and other holy books even give specific advice for how to do so.

In Hebrew, the word *tzedakah* refers to acts that we call "charity" in English—giving aid, support, and money to the poor and needy and worthy causes. But it's important to know too that the same Hebrew letters form the root words for both "charity" and "justice." Through Jewish eyes, charity is also about fairness and giving those less fortunate than you the same chances you have: It's an obligation not dependent on your mood.

There are different levels of charity in Judaism. Giving begrudgingly is considered the lowest level, but it's still better than giving nothing at all. What are the highest levels? Giving when nobody knows that you did—so you're not receiving praise or flattery—and giving in such a way that the recipient won't need charity anymore—such as helping someone get a job or learn a trade.

Behaving charitably makes us better people. It opens our hearts to the plight of others and helps us to see the world outside of our own circumstances. This broadening of our perspective allows us to feel empathy and appreciation for the things we are lucky enough to have, making us less selfish and self-centered. Rabbi Nachman of Bratslav two centuries ago advised that "it is good to give to charity before praying" and that "aiding the deserving saves us from sadness, laziness, and pride."

In Judaism, *tzedakah* doesn't mean only giving money to the needy, but also proactively caring for them. The Talmud relates that one of Rabbi Akiva's students once became very sick. Nobody came to visit except for Rabbi Akiva. Because he swept and cleaned the student's room, the student fully recovered. The student gratefully exclaimed to him, "Rabbi, you have given me life!" Rabbi Akiva then said, "Those who do not visit a sick person might just as well have spilled his or her blood."

live and learn

Does your family have any favorite charities? If so, what are they, and whom do these organizations help?

....

....

....

....

....

....

....

....

....

Most synagogues give money or other kinds of donations to charities. To what organizations does your synagogue contribute?

....

....

....

....

....

....

....

....

What services do Jewish charities provide in your area?

What charities, causes, or nonprofit organizations have you heard of that you are interested in learning more about?

How can you help someone or a particular cause without donating money? (For example, you could donate your time to help plant a community vegetable garden.)

The Bible (Proverbs 14:31) says, "A person who oppresses someone who is poor insults God." What does this mean to you?

making a difference

"How wonderful it is that nobody need wait a single moment before starting to improve the world." —Anne Frank

"Every individual has one's own challenges, assignments, and responsibility in the world" —Rabbi Moshe Chaim Luzzatto

תיקון עולם

You probably want to get started making a difference in your life, especially now that you've gained Jewish adulthood. You're not alone. More and more young people today seem to be feeling this way—perhaps because thanks to technology the world keeps getting smaller. We can bring almost the whole world into our homes as never before. As a result, we can more quickly—and clearly—see what needs to be done to make the globe a better place for all.

Judaism has always taught that we each should play a part in the adventure called *tikun ha'olam* (redeeming the world). We're not expected to finish the process of turning chaos into harmony, disorder into beauty and perfection—for that's really up to God. Rather, as *Pirkei Avot* says, we're only asked to further the process as best we can. But how? Exactly what should we do?

The Kabbalah teaches that we each have a unique mission on earth. In the words of the Baal Shem Tov, the founder of Hasidism, "No two persons have the same abilities. Each one should work in the service of God according to his or her own talents. If someone tries to imitate another, he or she merely loses the opportunity to do good things in his or her own way." His great-grandson, Rabbi Nachman of Bratslav, later boiled it down: "God does not do the same thing twice."

Knowing our personal mission in life isn't easy. Its nature will probably unfold gradually, over time: by meeting different people who will become important as helpers and guides, by traveling to new places, and by gaining knowledge and wisdom in school and other environments. None of this happens overnight, of course.

But you can start—right now—to find your mission by thinking about yourself deeply. Your interests, talents, and abilities are like arrows that God created for you to reach a certain mark with, and with which you can play your part in *tikun ha'olam*. They're also what give you joy in everyday life.

Learning to aim your arrows well will take practice, and will surely include mistakes, so be patient. You have the power from on high, and it's yours to use to benefit humanity.

live and learn

Name three things that you really enjoy doing and why you enjoy them.

1

2

3

What is your favorite Jewish thing to do, and how do you think it plays a part in tikun ha'olam?

Name a skill or talent that you have. How would you like to improve it?

What kind of job or type of work do you see yourself doing in the future? How will it help the world?

What could you do now to help make your goals come true?

Is there something—anything at all—you'd like to do now to make the world a better place? If so, what is it?

counting your blessings

"Who is happy? Those who are content with what they have."
—Pirkei Avot

ברכות

You've got a lot to be thankful for. You've now reached the age of adult status in Jewish life, and you're surrounded by the presence of loving family and friends. You also live in a country—unlike many others—that allows everybody, including Jews, to gather, worship, and celebrate in freedom. These are no small, meaningless things. They're fantastic. In many cases, though, we often don't feel especially grateful for these blessings and instead focus on what's *missing* in our lives.

But don't worry about it. This tendency is true for nearly everyone, young and old, and we've slipped into this forgetfulness time and again over thousands of years. This is precisely why our sages emphasize the importance of being happy with what we have and why they so strongly condemn the opposite—greed. But also in their view, the desire to want more and more is still a virulent tendency in human nature.

According to Jewish lore, this desire was even true for the wise King Solomon. Legend has it that he was cast down from his high position and forced to wander for several years as a tattered beggar because he had failed to be thankful to God. Only when Solomon truly appreciated what he *had*—instead of complaining about what he *lacked*—was his abundance restored to him. As the old Jewish proverb from Eastern Europe goes, "While pursuing happiness, we flee from contentment."

The Bible says that we're each made in God's image; that means that everyone has a higher soul that must grow and develop. Vital to that growth is learning to be thankful each day for the goodness we experience. So go to it!

live and learn

Think back since your last birthday. Name three things that you have experienced in the last year for which you are thankful.

1

2

3

Name three things that you learned about during your bar or bat mitzvah preparation that have made you thankful.

1

2

3

Now think back over your entire life. Name five things that you are thankful for:

1

2

3

4

5

You are wonderfully special to many people, like your family members and friends. Who are the people who consider you an important part of their lives?

meditation:

your higher connection

"Be still, and know that I am God." —Psalms 46:10

רוח הקודש

Becoming a bar or bat mitzvah brings you to a higher level of Jewish spirituality. Many new opportunities for growth now await you—including meditation. Meditation is such a valuable practice, because Judaism teaches that we are all born with a divine spark inside our souls, something that's intimately connected to God. That spark—known in Hebrew as *ruach hakodesh* (the holy spirit)—is inside every person, but sometimes it's hard for us to know it's there, even in ourselves.

Why? Because, as the sages commented, our chores and responsibilities often keep us so busy that we forget to look deeply within ourselves. We focus too much on unimportant things instead of the blessing and beauty in our lives. Stress can make this situation even worse. For this reason, our tradition has long offered many ways for us to calm ourselves and strengthen our bond with God. As Rabbi Nachman of Bratslav said about 200 years ago, "The days pass and are gone, and one finds that he or she never once had time to think. One who does not meditate cannot have wisdom."

There are many Jewish types of meditation. Some involve using the Hebrew alphabet, while others make use of Hebrew chants and songs or inspiring words and verses from the Bible. Some people use simple techniques, and some study more complex ways for years, but for most, meditating is always worth it. Many in the health-care community agree that meditation benefits our bodies as well as our minds. You can start now, at your age, on this exciting path. The next section gives some easy guidance for starting this Jewish tradition yourself.

live and learn

Name a place—it could be from summer camp or a family vacation spot—where you felt really relaxed.

What made this place so relaxing to you?

Now close your eyes for a few minutes and imagine yourself being there. What is the easiest thing to imagine?

Relax your body. Close your eyes and let your lips close lightly. As you breathe through your nose, notice the air's flow in and out of your nostrils. For a few minutes, just be aware of this gentle flow. Feel how calm you now are. Did you think of anything while you did this? If so, what did you think about it?

Choose any Hebrew letter, such as the first letter of your Hebrew name; page 36 has a list of all the letters. Draw the letter on large, blank paper and place it before you. As you sit, look silently at the letter for about a minute. Notice its shape in every detail you can. Then, close your eyes and see the letter in your mind. Does the letter remind you of anything? Does it evoke particular feelings? If so, write down as many things as you can.

Paste the piece of paper with the letter on it here. Or, you may wish to just keep it in this journal loosely so you can use it again.

your synagogue ceremony

עליה

The bar or bat mitzvah ceremony at the synagogue service is the religious heart of your big day. This celebratory coming-of-age has been common since the Middle Ages, and it initiates you to the core ritual of Jewish adulthood: entering the circle of public prayer. For the first time, you can be counted in a *minyan* (the group of ten adults that make up a public quorum) and to be called for an *aliyah* (the privilege of reciting the blessings over the reading of the Torah).

These acts symbolize your ability to stand with adults and to carry tradition forward into a new generation, and they are crucial parts of your bar or bat mitzvah ceremony, as are reading some or all of the weekly Torah portion, chanting the *haftarah* portion (the weekly reading from the Prophets), and sometimes leading the congregation in prayer. And nearly all of you give a *devar torah*, or speech, in which you offer personal wisdom and gratitude for your Jewish coming-of-age.

It's probably the most important speech of your life thus far, in which you express your thoughts before people who know and love you. You've surely spent a lot of careful time on what to say. And if you've chosen to interpret your Torah or *haftarah* portion, that's doubly wonderful—the Holy Book has sustained our people throughout many generations.

Although the Holy Book dates back thousands of years, you've probably found your portions have meaning in today's world as well. And that's not surprising. Our sages have always insisted on the Torah's timelessness. As an old Jewish saying affirms, "Israel, Torah, and God are one."

live and learn

At what synagogue did your bar or bat mitzvah take place?

Address

What does the name of your synagogue mean in English if its name is in Hebrew?

Who was the rabbi that presided over your ceremony?

Who was the cantor?

Who led the synagogue service?

Who was honored with an invitation to recite the *aliyot*?

Did you recite any particular prayers on your own? Which ones?

What was your Torah portion (in Hebrew and English)?

What was your portion about?

What was your *haftarah* portion (in Hebrew and English)?

What was your portion about?

What was your *devar torah* about? Describe in a few sentences, or paste a copy of the actual speech here.

Who recited the *kiddush* after the service?

Who said the *hamotzi*?

What was your favorite part of the ceremony?

Did you have any special songs or sayings at your ceremony? What were they?

Paste the invitation to your bar or bat mitzvah here.

celebrating the big day

חגיגה

To celebrate the big day, some people have small family gatherings like a dinner or kiddush lunch. Others prefer to have bigger parties. Whatever the size of your affair, here's a place to record some of its most memorable moments.

Where was your celebration held?

Who came the longest distance to be at your celebration?

Which family or families had the most people attending your celebration?

Who sat next to you at your celebration?

Did you have a candle-lighting ceremony? If so, who was called up to participate?

Who said the *kiddush*?

Who cut the challah and led the *hamotzi*?

What were your favorite Jewish songs played at your celebration?

Did you do any favorite Jewish dances, such as the hora?

What other favorite songs of yours played at your celebration?

Did anyone give a speech or toast at your celebration? If so, who?
What did they say?

Paste some pictures here of your favorite moments of the celebration.

a letter to God

מכתב לאלוהים

Your bar or bat mitzvah celebration is now over, but it's still fresh in your mind. And so are the excitement and joy in the hearts of your parents, grandparents, relatives, and friends. Your coming of age into Jewish adult responsibility is truly a memorable and blessed event. But as our sages knew, memories fade and must be actively recalled by our words and acts. Indeed, that's the purpose of this book. So while you're still basking in the glow of your celebration—and before starting the thank-you notes for gifts—take a little time now to think about what it all means. How? By writing a letter to God.

Don't worry. You aren't being graded on what you say, and you don't have to be a sage or a prophet to be sincere. Rather, be yourself. In the space provided here, jot down a few sentences that will help this wonderful event remain bright in your soul.

Here are a few suggestions for your letter: First, what would you like to *thank* God for? This can include your preparation and study, your actual synagogue ceremony, and the encouragement you received from loved ones and friends. You can name specific people and thank God for bringing them into your life at this time. Second, what did you *learn* about yourself in the past months leading up to your bar or bat mitzvah? Perhaps you found that you have strengths and abilities that you didn't appreciate—or didn't even realize were there. If so, let God know about this, too. Finally, what are your hopes for the future? Now that you're an adult in Jewish responsibility, how can God join you to make the world a better place? Remember, Judaism teaches that we're each responsible for what we personally do, but God is always present, too. So how would you like God's help to be the best person you can?